Bible Wisdom for Gen Z: Proverbs for Life

CONTENTS

Bible Wisdom for Gen Z: Proverbs for Life

CHAPTER I. SOLOMON'S LIFE HACKS

INTRO TO WINNING AT LIFE

Let's break down these ancient texts from Solomon, David's son, and the king of Israel. These words are all about leveling up in wisdom, discipline, and understanding. It's like a guidebook for living a solid life, filled with integrity, justice, and straight-up honesty.

He's talking straight to the youth, saying, "Listen up, I'm gonna level up your brain game." This is for everyone, from noobs to vets. Tune into his wisdom playlist, and you're on the express lane to being savvy and untangling life's complex puzzles.

THE BASICS OF BEING WISE

The ground floor of getting wise is giving props to the Big Guy upstairs—that's the cornerstone. Miss this, and you're stumbling right out of the gate. Solomon's not just talking the talk; he's the guidebook away from the shady deals and bad calls. He's like, "When the bad crowd tries to pull you into their mess, just ghost them. It's a one-way trip to nowhere good."

WISDOM'S STREET CRED

Picture wisdom as the cool influencer in the town square,

shouting out to anyone who'll listen, handing out the roadmap to everything legit. Wisdom's on blast, saying, "Stop chasing shadows. I've got the hookup to the real deal."

DISSING WISDOM: EPIC FAIL

Here's the breakdown: ignore wisdom, and when the bottom falls out, wisdom's gonna hit you with an "I told you so." Ignore the call? Don't expect a lifeline when the storm hits.

THE SMOOTH PATH VS.
THE BUMPY ROAD

Final score: Listen to wisdom for that smooth journey, zero drama. Skip the wisdom track, and you're asking for trouble.

So, that's the lowdown from the wisdom vault. It's all about making smart choices, respecting the grind, and steering clear of trouble. Wisdom's calling out - it's on you to answer.

CHAPTER II. BENEFITS OF SEEKING WISDOM

THE CHEAT CODE

Listen up, if you grab onto my lessons and keep my commands locked down, if you lean in close to wisdom and tune your heart to understanding, calling out for insight like you're shouting from the rooftops, and if you start hunting for it like it's the ultimate treasure, then you're in for a real game-changer.

DISCOVERING THE FEAR OF THE BIG BOSS

You'll unlock the ultimate respect for the Big Boss upstairs and get VIP access to understanding Him. That's because the Boss himself dishes out wisdom, along with knowledge and insight straight from His own lips. He's got a security detail for the straight shooters and acts like a shield for those who play fair.

GETTING THE INSIDE TRACK

He's all about protecting the path of justice and guarding the way of His loyal crew. You'll get the inside track on what's right, just, and fair, and every good path will start to make sense. Wisdom will take up residence in your heart, and knowledge will be your new best friend. Thoughtfulness will keep a lookout for you, and discernment will have your back.

STEERING CLEAR OF TROUBLE...

It's your ticket out of trouble's way, away from the talkers who twist the truth, from those who've ditched the straight and narrow for the back alleys of bad decisions—those who think messing up is a sport and thrive on twisted paths.

...ESPECIALLY FROM THAT TOXIC RELATIONSHIP

It's your shield against getting tangled up with someone else's significant other, the one who forgot the promises they made and is headed straight for a dead-end. Anyone who goes that way doesn't come back; they never find the road to real life again.

RACKING UP THE BLESSINGS

So, you'll walk the path of the good guys, stick to the routes of the righteous. Because the upstanding folks will have the world at their feet, and the honest ones will fill it up. But the wicked? They'll be wiped off the map, roots and all.

CHAPTER III. STAY TIGHT WITH GOD!

CALLING OUT

Hey there, keep my teachings close to your heart, they're like the secret sauce for a life well-lived. Wrap love and loyalty around you like your favorite chain, etch them deep inside, and watch how you gain favor and props from both the divine and folks around.

TRUST IN THE DIVINE

Put your whole heart into trusting the divine, don't rely just on your own smarts. Keep the divine in your thoughts no matter where you're headed, and watch your path smooth out.

RESPECT THE DIVINE

Don't get too big for your britches. Show respect, steer clear of trouble, and it's like a health boost for your body and a refresh for your spirit.

DIVINE CONTRIBUTIONS

Show some love with what you've got, give back from the top of your stash, and you'll see your resources overflow and your vats brimming with the good stuff.

TAKE THE GUIDANCE

Don't shrug off divine discipline, my dude. The divine corrects those loved, just as a parent guides a child who is cherished.

WISDOM: THE ULTIMATE LOOT

Blessed are those who get wisdom, who grab hold of understanding. It's a better grab than silver, more profitable than gold, and beats pearls for value. Wisdom's got longevity and wealth in both hands, walking paths of pleasure and leading ways to peace. Holding onto wisdom is grabbing life itself, bringing joy to its friends. The world's foundation? Laid down with wisdom. The skies? Set in place with understanding. It's the key to the deep and the morning dew.

STAY ALERT

So, keep wisdom and insight in your sights, they're life to your soul and a sweet look for you. Walk safe, don't trip; when you rest, no nightmares, and you'll sleep tight. No need to fear sudden disasters or the comeuppance of the wicked, because the divine's got your back, protecting you from getting caught in the trap.

SOCIAL TIPS

Don't hold back on doing good when it's in your power to act. Don't tell your neighbor to "hit me up later" if you can help now. Don't plot against those living their life worry-free. Avoid needless beefs, especially if they've done you no harm.

DIVINE PAYBACK

Don't envy those who do wrong; their ways are not for you. The divine can't stand twisted folks but pours out love to those walking straight. The twisted get cursed, but the righteous get blessed. The divine throws shade at mockers but gives grace to the humble. The wise inherit honor, but fools get nothing but shame.

CHAPTER IV. LEVEL UP YOUR WISDOM GAME

EPIC LOOT OF WISDOM

Yo, kids, listen up to your old man's advice, if you wanna get wise, you gotta tune in! I'm dropping some serious knowledge: don't ghost my guidance, okay?

Back in the day, I was just like you, chilling with my dad, the apple of my mom's eye, and here's what he schooled me: "Lock these words in your heart, follow my commands and live; go all out for wisdom, go all out for understanding, don't forget what I say, and don't diss wisdom! If you love her, she's got your back; embrace her, and she'll look out for you.

Starting point of wisdom: Get wisdom, at all costs, get understanding! Treasure her, and she'll elevate you; she'll honor you if you embrace her; she'll gift you a stunning crown, a glorious crown she'll bestow on you."

WHY WISDOM'S PATH ROCKS

Hear me out, kiddo, soak up my words, and you'll level up your life. I'll guide you in the wisdom zone, lead you down paths of righteousness. When you walk this path, your steps won't be hindered, and if you sprint, you won't stumble. Hold onto instruction, don't let it go; guard it well, it's your life, dude.

PATH OF THE WICKED = HARD PASS

Don't even step on the path of the wicked, don't go down the road of bad vibes; avoid it, don't travel on it, turn away from it and pass on by. For they don't sleep unless they've done wrong; they're robbed of sleep unless they make someone stumble. For they feast on wickedness and guzzle down violence. But the path of the righteous is like the first gleam of dawn, shining ever brighter till the full light of day. The way of the wicked is deep darkness; they don't know what makes them stumble.

WISDOM = YOUR BESTIE

Pay attention, my child, to what I say; turn your ear to my words. Don't lose sight of them, keep them within your heart; for they are life to those who find them and health to one's whole body. Guard your heart above all else, for it determines the course of your life. Avoid dishonest talk, keep your lips away from deceit. Let your eyes look straight ahead; fix your gaze directly before you. Give careful thought to the paths for your feet and be steadfast in all your ways. Do not turn to the right or the left; keep your foot from evil.

CHAPTER V. CHEATING VS LOYALTY: KEEPING IT REAL

WATCH OUT FOR THE OTHER WOMAN

Yo, listen up! Tune into wisdom and keep your ears open for some real talk. Stay sharp and don't let your guard down. That smooth talk from someone not yours? It's sweet like honey now but ends up bitter, leading you down a path to nowhere good. Keep your eyes on your own path, cherish what's yours.

THE FALLOUT OF STEPPING OUT

Heads up, don't stray from these life lessons. Steer clear from doors that aren't yours to open. You don't want to end up giving away your best years to those who don't deserve it, filling someone else's pockets with your hard-earned goods. In the end, you'll only have regrets and "what ifs." Stay wise, stay on track.

KEEPING IT FAITHFUL

Drink from your own well, cherish the love you've built. Why look elsewhere when you've got real treasure at home? Dive deep into the love that's been yours from the start. Find joy and peace right where you are, with the one who's been by your side all along.

THE DOWNSIDE OF WRONG TURNS

Every step you take, it's all under the watchful eyes above. Taking the wrong path? It's a surefire way to tie yourself up in knots you can't untangle. Ignoring wisdom's call, you'll find yourself lost, wandering off into a mess with no way back.

CHAPTER VI. STAY SMART, AVOID DEBT TRAPS

BEWARE OF CO-SIGNING

Yo, if you ever put your name down for someone else's debt, listen up! You've locked yourself in with just a handshake. So hustle, get out of it by any means necessary—like a deer escaping a hunter or a bird from a trap.

LAZY DAYS, EMPTY POCKETS

Ever watched ants? No boss, yet they stock up food like pros. What's your excuse for hitting the snooze button? Wake up, or poverty will sneak up on you like a thief—sudden and unwelcome.

THE TROUBLE WITH TROUBLEMAKERS

Some folks are just bad news: lying, scheming, always stirring the pot. Their end comes quick, a disaster they can't dodge. And yep, there are things even the Big Guy upstairs can't stand: arrogance, lies, violence, plotting evil, rushing into wrongdoing, lying under oath, and sowing discord.

LISTENING PAYS OFF

Hang tight to your parents' teachings; they're your lifeline. They'll guide you, protect you, and speak to you even in your sleep. They're the light that shows you the way to live right.

THE DANGER ZONE OF CHEATING

That sweet talk from someone else's partner might seem tempting, but it's a one-way ticket to trouble. It'll cost you more than you can afford, leading to regret and ruin. Don't even get close. Remember, the Lord sees everything. Go down that path, and you're playing with fire, literally. Cheating doesn't just burn; it destroys.

KEEPING IT REAL

Keep your parents' wisdom close. It's your necklace of life, guiding you away from making a bad call. And about stepping out on your partner? Just don't. It's a mess you can't clean, a wound that won't heal, and a price too high to pay. Stay wise, stay faithful. It's worth it.

CHAPTER VII. BEWARE OF THE SEDUCER

A WARNING FOR THE YOUNG

Yo, keep my words close and my commands even closer. Guard them like the apple of your eye. Tie them around your finger, write them on the tablet of your heart. Call wisdom your sister, make understanding your BFF, to keep you away from the stranger with the smooth talk.

THE DANGER LURKS

Peeking out my window, I saw among the clueless, spotted a young dude totally lacking sense. He was walking down her street, headed straight for her corner, in the twilight, in the evening, under the cover of night.

THE TRAP SET

And there she was, dressed to kill, with sneaky intentions, loud and stubborn, her feet never staying home. Now in the streets, now in the squares, lurking at every corner.

THE TEMPTATION

She grabbed him, kissed him, with a brazen face she said, "I had to offer sacrifices, today I fulfilled my vows. So I came out to meet you, looking for you, and here you are! I've decked out my bed with colorful linens from Egypt, perfumed my bed with myrrh, aloes, and cinnamon. Come, let's drink deep of love till morning; let's enjoy ourselves with love. My husband's not home, he's gone on a long journey. He took his money bag with him; he won't be home till the full moon."

THE FALL

With her persuasive speech, she led him astray; with her smooth talk, she seduced him. All at once he followed her, like an ox going to the slaughter, like a deer stepping into a noose till an arrow pierces its liver, like a bird darting into a snare, not knowing it will cost him his life.

THE CAUTION

Now, sons, listen to me; pay attention to what I say. Do not let your heart turn to her ways or stray into her paths. Many are the victims she has brought down; her slain are a mighty throng. Her house is a highway to the grave, leading down to the chambers of death.

CHAPTER VIII. WISDOM SHOUTS OUT

WISDOM'S CALLOUT

Wisdom's shouting out, you know? Understanding's raising her voice too. At the top spot, by the road, at the crossroads, she's just chilling. By the gates, at the city's entry, in the doorways, she's making herself heard: "I'm talking to all y'all, calling out to humanity. You guys who don't get it, learn some wisdom. You fools, get a grip on some sense.

Listen up, I'm dropping important stuff here, speaking nothing but the truth. Hate lies, love honesty. All my words are straight-up, no room for deceit. If you've got brains, you'll see they're all clear, and right on if you've got knowledge. Choose my teaching over silver, knowledge over the finest gold. 'Cause wisdom's worth more than rubies, and all the bling you could want doesn't compare."

WISDOM'S BENEFITS

I'm Wisdom, got Insight living right next door, knowledge and deep thought are my roomies. Respecting the Lord means hating evil. Pride, arrogance, bad behavior, and twisted speech, I can't stand. I've got good advice and common sense, I've got insight, I've got power. By me, kings reign, rulers make laws that are just. By me, leaders rule, and nobles make all the right decisions. Love me, and I'll love you back. Seek me out, and you'll find me.

With me, you'll find riches and honor, enduring wealth and justice. My rewards are better than gold, even the pure stuff, and my returns beat the best silver. I walk the path of righteousness, take the road of justice, giving wealth to those who love me, filling their houses with treasures.

CREATOR'S COMPANION

The Lord created me at the beginning, His first work, long ago. I was formed before everything, before the earth itself. I was born before the oceans, before the springs filled with water. Before the mountains were settled, before the hills, I came to life.

Before God made the land or fields, or any of the dust of the earth. I was there when He set up the heavens, when He drew the horizon on the ocean. I was there when He hung the clouds and made the springs of the deep strong. I was there when He set the limits for the sea, when He laid out the foundations of the earth. I was the master worker, always delighted in His presence, having a blast playing in His world, and delighting in humanity.

FINAL WORDS

So, my children, listen to me. Those who stick to my ways are happy. Listen to my instruction and be wise. Don't ignore it. Blessed is the one who listens to me, watching daily at my doors, waiting at my doorway. For those who find me find life and receive favor from the Lord. But those who miss out on me injure themselves. All who hate me love death."

CHAPTER IX. WISDOM'S FEAST

INVITING THE GUESTS

Wisdom's built her crib, carved out seven pillars, whipped up a feast, mixed some wine, and set the table. She sent out her crew to shout from the city's high spots: "Yo, if you're clueless, swing by my way." To anyone lacking in smarts, she's like: "Come over, feast on my bread, sip on the wine I mixed. Ditch ignorance and live, step onto the path of insight."

NO POINT SCHOOLING THE SCOFFER

Schooling a mocker just earns you disdain, call out a hater and you'll just hurt yourself. Don't bother correcting those who mock, they'll hate you for it; but correct the wise, they'll love you for it. Teach the wise, and they get wiser; enlighten the enlightened, they'll gain more insight.

THE BLESSING OF WISDOM

The essence of wisdom? Fear of the Lord. Knowing the Holy One? That's real understanding. With me, your days will multiply, and more years will be added to your life. If you're wise, you're doing yourself a solid; mock wisdom, and you're the one who'll pay.

FOLLY'S FEAST

Lady Folly's loud, clueless, knows nothing. Perched at her crib's door, on a seat at the city's heights, calling out to those minding their own biz, straight-up walking their path: "Hey, inexperienced ones, this way!" To the clueless, she's like: "Stolen water's sweet, and bread eaten in secret is tasty." But they don't know that the dead hang at her pad, that her guests are deep in the grave.

CHAPTER X. LIFE HACKS: WISDOM WINS

Yo, listen up, here's some solid advice from
the wisdom vault of Solomon:

A smart kid makes their dad proud, but a foolish
one is a total facepalm for their mom.

Chasing bad money gets you nowhere, but doing
the right thing can save your skin.

The Big Guy upstairs won't let the good folks go hungry,
but He's got no time for the wicked's wish list.

Laziness gets you broke, while hard work fills your pockets.

A wise child is all about that harvest life,
sleeping through it is just shameful.

Blessings rain down on the good guys, but the bad
ones? They're just asking for trouble.

Remembering a good person feels awesome, but the wicked?
They'll be forgotten faster than your last Snapchat.

Wisdom sinks in for the smart at heart, but saying
dumb stuff is a fast track to failure.

Living right means living safe. Taking shady
shortcuts will only get you exposed.

Wink and nudge towards trouble, and you're going down.
Speak nonsense, and it's a faceplant waiting to happen.

Truth and life flow from the lips of the good, but violence? That's the bad guys' language.

Hate stirs up drama, but love covers up all the mess-ups.

Wisdom is what smart lips talk about, but a lack of smarts gets you nowhere fast.

The rich have their wealth as their fortress, but poverty spells doom for the poor.

Doing right earns you a lifetime pass, but wrongdoing pays back in full.

Listening to advice means you're on the way to life; ignore it, and you're headed off the cliff.

Spreading hate is a no-go, but being a blabbermouth is just plain dumb.

Talk too much, and you're bound to mess up; keep it wise, and you stay smart.

The right words are pure gold, but the wicked's heart? Worthless.

Righteous peeps guide many to safety, but fools crash and burn in their own cluelessness.

God's blessing makes you rich without adding sorrow.

Fools get their kicks from doing dumb stuff, but for the wise, wisdom is the way to go.

What the wicked dread will overtake them, but the righteous get their heart's desire.

When the storm hits, the wicked vanish, but the righteous have an eternal foundation.

Just like vinegar to teeth and smoke to eyes, so are the lazy to those who send them.

Keeping it cool with God adds years to your life,
but the wicked? Their time is cut short.

The good peeps look forward to happiness, but
the wicked's hopes will bite the dust.

God's got the back of those doing right, but the
wrongdoers? They're heading straight for disaster.

The righteous stand tall forever, but the wicked
won't last long on this earth.

Wisdom should flow from the lips of the just,
but twisted tongues will be silenced.

Honest lips dig what's right, but the deceitful?
They're all about the twist.

CHAPTER XI. VIBES DON'T LIE

Gross to the Divine is a shady scale, but an
honest weight is where it's at.

Pride walks in, disgrace follows, but humility
is where wisdom hangs.

Honesty paves the way for the righteous, but the
deceitful fall hard by their own wickedness.

When trouble hits, riches won't save you, but
righteousness pulls you through.

The innocence of the just makes their path straight,
but the wicked fall by their own wickedness.

Righteousness saves the upright, but
cravings ensnare the wicked.

When a sinner's ticket is up, their hope turns to
dust, and the twisted's expectations go poof.

The righteous get pulled from trouble, but
the wicked take their place.

The wicked's words aim to destroy, but the
insight of the upright saves the day.

The city celebrates when the righteous thrive, and
joy erupts when the wicked are no more.

A city rises on the blessings of the upright, but
the wicked's mouth tears it down.

Looking down on others is foolish, but the
wise keep it on the down low.

A gossip spills the beans, but a trustworthy
spirit keeps it under wraps.

Without guidance, people fall, but in the
counsel of many, there's safety.

Guaranteeing someone else's debt can be trouble,
but avoiding such binds keeps you safe.

A graceful woman gains honor, and the brave stack up wealth.

Kindness works in your favor, but cruelty
torments its own master.

The unjust get a fleeting gain, but sowing
righteousness reaps a sure reward.

Heading towards life is the righteous man, but
chasing sin leads straight to death.

The Divine can't stand twisted hearts, but loves
those walking the straight line.

Evil won't go unpunished, but the descendants
of the righteous will be safe.

A gold ring in a pig's snout is a beautiful
woman without discretion.

The righteous desire only good, but the wicked brace for rage.

One gives freely and grows richer, while
the over-tight end up in want.

A generous person thrives, and the one who
waters will also be watered.

People curse those hoarding their grain,
but bless the one selling it.

Doing good seeks favor; chasing evil, it hits back.

Trusting in wealth is a fast track to a fall, but
the righteous flourish like leaves.

Disturbing one's own house inherits wind, and
a fool becomes servant to the wise.

The fruit of the righteous is a tree of life, and wisdom wins souls.

If the righteous get their due on earth, how
much more the wicked and the sinner.

CHAPTER XII. REAL TALK: WISDOM VS. FOOLISHNESS

Digging wisdom means you're into learning;
hating correction is just plain dumb.

Good vibes find favor with the Divine, but schemers
catch a one-way ticket to Nopeville.

Wrongdoing won't keep you standing; the
righteous have roots that don't budge.

A strong partner is a crown; a shameless one is just decay.

Righteous folks plan with integrity; schemers
always got a trick up their sleeve.

The words of the faithless are traps; honest
talk can save your skin.

When the wicked fall, it's game over, but the
righteous? Their home stands strong.

Wisdom gets you respect; twisty paths lead to disdain.

Better to hustle quietly than boast with nothing in your pocket.

Caring for your crew shows you're straight;
cold hearts are just cruel.

Work the land, you'll have your fill; chase
fantasies, you're off your rocker.

The wicked look for cover in chaos; the

righteous stand tall and secure.

Your own words can trap you; the straight
shooter dodges disaster.

What you say feeds you; your hustle pays back.

Fools think they're always right; wise ones consider advice.

Anger shows fast on a fool; the wise brush off insults.

Truth-tellers speak justice; liars deal in deceit.

Reckless words cut deep; wise words can heal.

Truth lasts forever; lies are here today, gone tomorrow.

No harm comes to the good; the wicked's world is full of trouble.

The Divine can't stand liars; truth-speakers are the real MVPs.

Wise folks keep knowledge on the DL; fools broadcast nonsense.

Hard work leads to power; laziness ends in hard labor.

A heavy heart drags you down; a kind word lifts you up.

The righteous might choose differently but end up
better off; the wicked's way leads to ruin.

Laziness doesn't catch dinner; diligence is priceless.

Walking the path of righteousness is life
itself; staying on it is eternal.

CHAPTER XIII. PRO TIPS FOR THE WISE

A smart kid digs getting feedback; a mocker won't even listen.

You reap what you sow – good vibes bring good life;
deceit fills you up with nothing but trouble.

Guard your words, protect your life; speak without
thinking, and it's your own downfall.

Dreaming gets the lazy nowhere; hard
work makes dreams happen.

The upright can't stand twisted talk; the
wicked thrive on causing trouble.

Integrity paves a safe path; wickedness trips up the wrongdoer.

Pretending to be rich with nothing is pointless; it's
better to be poor and have real wealth.

Wealth can't save you when times get tough;
only righteousness pulls you through.

The good-hearted live a bright life; the faithless
only have their light dimmed.

Arrogance only leads to conflict; wisdom is
found by those who seek advice.

Ill-gotten gains vanish; slow and steady builds wealth that lasts.

Waiting too long is a heartache; a dream

come true is a breath of fresh air.

Ignoring guidance leads to trouble; following
instructions brings a reward.

Wisdom's lessons are a fountain of life,
steering you clear from danger.

Sensible people win respect; the path of
the treacherous is slippery.

The wise weigh their actions; fools flaunt their foolishness.

A dodgy messenger falls into trouble;
trustworthiness is a healing balm.

Ignoring correction leads to poverty and shame;
heeding reproof brings honor.

A fulfilled desire soothes the soul; turning
from evil is too much for a fool.

Hang with the wise and get wiser; a fool's buddy gets into trouble.

Misfortune hunts down sinners; the righteous
are rewarded with good.

A good person leaves an inheritance for the grandkids;
sinners' wealth ends up in the hands of the good.

Hard work of the poor yields plenty; unjust gain dwindles away.

Spare the rod, hate your kid; love them, discipline them timely.

The righteous never go hungry; the wicked
stomach remains empty.

CHAPTER XIV. BUILDING WISDOM, DODGING FOLLY

A wise chick builds her nest, while foolishness wrecks it solo.

Living right vibes with fearing the Lord, but
the crooked can't stand Him.

Fools' mouths land them in trouble, but the wise keep it cool.

No oxen, no grain; strong oxen, big gains.

Truth-tellers don't lie, fakers spread deceit.

Mockers chasing wisdom get nowhere, but
the smart catch on quick.

Steer clear of fools; you won't find wisdom there.

Smart peeps navigate their path; fools deceive themselves.

Wrongdoing hooks fools, but the righteous ride on grace.

Only you feel your own pain, joy's a solo trip too.

Traitors' houses crumble, but the righteous tent blooms.

Some roads seem right but end in a nosedive.

Laughter can hide a heartache; joy sometimes ends in sorrow.

The faithless feed on their mischief, but the
righteous savor their deeds.

Fools buy everything they hear, but the wise watch their step.

Fear the bad, bail fast; fools rush in and regret.

Hot-headed peeps make messes, the cunning get no love.

Gullibility lands you in trouble, but being
smart dresses you in success.

The bad bow before the good, the wicked
at the gates of the righteous.

Poor folks lack friends, the rich never short of a crowd.

Dissing your peeps is straight-up wrong; blessed
are those who care for the poor.

Plotting evil leads you astray, but love and
truth for those with good intent.

Hard work pays off; talk is cheap.

Skills crown the wise; folly is the fool's crown.

Honest witnesses save lives; lies just spread more lies.

Fear of the Lord is a safe haven; His kids find refuge in Him.

Revering the Lord is life's fountain, dodging death's traps.

A king shines with a big crowd; a leader falls without followers.

Patience is golden; impulsiveness shows folly.

A calm heart is life for the body; envy rots the bones.

Oppressing the poor insults their Maker; honoring
Him means caring for the needy.

Wickedness takes down the sinner; the
righteous chill even in death.

Wisdom chills in the wise heart, fools should take note.

Justice lifts a nation; sin drags it down.

Kings dig sensible servants; they're not fans of disgrace.

CHAPTER XV. CHILL VIBES AND WISE LIVES

A chill response turns down the heat, while
harsh words stir up anger.

From the wise, knowledge flows like a stream;
foolishness is all that bursts from fools' mouths.

The Lord's got eyes everywhere, keeping
tabs on both the good and bad.

A gentle tongue is a life-giving tree, but a
twisted one breaks the spirit.

Ignoring your dad's advice is foolish, but
listening up is straight-up smart.

A righteous crib is full of treasure, but a
sinner's gains bring trouble.

Wise lips spread knowledge, but fools' hearts are unstable.

The Lord can't stand the offerings of the wicked,
but honest prayers are His jam.

Wicked paths are a no-go for the Lord, but He's all
about those who walk in righteousness.

Ignoring discipline gets you nowhere fast;
hate correction, and it's game over.

Even death and destruction don't phase the Lord,
so imagine how well He knows us!

Mockers hate being corrected, so they don't hang with the wise.

A happy heart makes for a beaming face, but
heartache crushes the spirit.

The inquisitive heart seeks knowledge, but fools feed on folly.

For the down-and-out, every day is a bad day, but
a cheerful heart has a never-ending party.

Better a little with respect for the Lord
than a fortune with turmoil.

A simple meal with love beats a feast with hate.

A hot-tempered person stirs up conflict, but
the patient one calms a quarrel.

The path of the lazy is like a thorny hedge, but
the way of the upright is a highway.

A wise son brings joy to his father, but a
foolish one is his mother's grief.

Folly delights the senseless, but the sensible
stay on the straight and narrow.

Without advice, plans fall apart, but with
many counselors, they succeed.

The right word at the right time is pure gold.

For the wise, life's a climb that keeps you from the grave.

Pride's house is destined for demolition, but the
Lord secures the widow's boundaries.

Evil plots are toxic to the Lord, but pure words are pristine.

Corruption in the house brings it down, but
integrity keeps you standing.

A righteous heart thinks before speaking;
wicked mouths spew hostility.

The Lord keeps His distance from the wicked,
but He hears the righteous' prayers.

Bright eyes gladden the heart; good news
gives health to the bones.

Listening to life-giving advice puts you among the wise.

Ignoring advice is self-sabotage, but following it brings wisdom.

Fear of the Lord is the beginning of wisdom,
and humility comes before honor.

CHAPTER XVI. HEARTFELT PLANS VS. DIVINE DECISIONS

Your heart might plot the course, but the
final say is from the Lord.

We all think we're in the clear, but it's the
Lord who checks the spirit.

Trust your hustle to the Lord, and your plans will thrive.

The Lord's got a reason for everything, even
setting up the wicked for a downfall.

Arrogance is a no-go for the Lord, and it
won't escape punishment.

Love and loyalty erase mistakes; fearing the
Lord keeps you off the wrong path.

If the Lord digs your vibe, He'll even make your enemies play nice.

Better to have a little with justice than
make a killing the wrong way.

You plan your journey, but the Lord determines your steps.

Kings speak divine, their verdicts don't miss.

The scales and weights are the Lord's department,
every measure is His call.

Kings hate wrongdoing, because justice
is the throne's foundation.

Honest talk is music to a king's ears, they
love those who speak the truth.

A king's wrath spells doom, but a wise man will chill it out.

A king's smile means life, like the refreshing spring rain.

Go for wisdom over gold, understanding over silver.

Staying away from evil is the way to go for
the righteous, it keeps you safe.

Pride comes before a fall, humility before honor.

Better to be humble among the lowly than
to share plunder with the proud.

Happy is the one who keeps the commands,
blessed are those who trust in the Lord.

A wise heart is known as understanding, and
sweet talk increases learning.

Wisdom is a life source for those who have it, but
foolishness is a punishment for fools.

Wise hearts make mouths smart, their lips spread insight.

Kind words are like honey, sweet to the
soul and healing to the bones.

Some paths seem right, but end in death.

Worker's hunger works for him; it drives him on.

A wicked person brews evil, their lips are like a scorching fire.

Deceivers stir up conflict, gossip separates close friends.

A violent person lures their neighbor, leading
them down a harmful path.

Who winks plots deceit; who purses their lips is bent on evil.

Grey hair is a crown of splendor, found on
the path of righteousness.

Patience beats strength, self-control over conquering a city.

Lots are cast into the lap, but every decision is from the Lord.

CHAPTER XVII. CHILL VIBES VS. DRAMA FEASTS

Chill bread crust beats a house full of feasting with drama.

A smart servant will outclass a shameful
son and inherit a family legacy.

The crucible is for silver, and the furnace for gold,
but the heart is tested by the vibes it holds.

Wrongdoers listen to twisted words, tricksters tune into deceit.

Mocking the poor insults their Maker; gloating
over disaster won't go unpunished.

Grandparents' crowns are their grandkids;
parents are the pride of their children.

Fancy words don't suit a fool, much less lying lips a leader.

A gift works like a charm for the giver;
wherever they turn, they succeed.

Seeking love covers over faults; spreading
gossip separates close friends.

A wise correction impacts a wise person more
than a hundred lashes a fool.

A rebel seeks only evil, so a cruel messenger
will be sent against them.

Better to meet a robbed mama bear than a fool in their folly.

Repaying good with evil, evil won't leave your house.

Starting a fight is like breaching a dam; drop
the argument before it escalates.

Both freeing the guilty and punishing the
innocent disgust the Lord.

What's the point of money in the hand of a fool to
buy wisdom when they have no sense?

A friend loves at all times, and a brother is born for adversity.

Guaranteeing a debt for another is senseless; it's a trap.

Loving conflict is loving sin; raising your
gate high invites destruction.

A crooked heart finds no good, and the
twisted tongue falls into trouble.

A fool's parent has grief; a fool's father has no joy.

A happy heart makes the face cheerful, but
heartache crushes the spirit.

The wise heart seeks knowledge, but fools feed on folly.

Better a little with the fear of the Lord than
great treasure with turmoil.

A small serving of vegetables with love is better
than a fattened calf with hatred.

A hot-tempered person stirs up conflict, but
the patient calms a quarrel.

The path of the lazy is blocked with thorns, but
the road of the upright is a highway.

A wise son brings joy to his father, but a
foolish son grief to his mother.

Folly is joy to one who lacks sense, but a person
with understanding walks straight.

Without counsel plans fail, but with many advisers they succeed.

A person finds joy in giving an apt reply
— and how good is a timely word!

The path of life leads upward for the wise to
avoid going down to the grave.

The Lord tears down the house of the proud, but he
sets the widow's boundary stones in place.

The Lord detests the thoughts of the wicked, but
gracious words are pure in his sight.

Whoever ignores discipline despises themselves, but
whoever heeds correction gains understanding.

The fear of the Lord teaches wisdom, and
humility comes before honor.

CHAPTER XVIII. LIFE'S ECHOES: VIBES AND CLASHES

Chasing their own vibe, some roll solo,
battling every piece of advice.

Thinking is a chore for the clueless, they're
all about airing their own views.

Shame follows the wicked, hand in hand with disgrace.

Deep talks are like a refreshing stream, wisdom
flows like an endless dream.

Backing the guilty, sidelining the just, that's
a no-go in the court of trust.

Fool's lips are a ticket to drama, their own words a call for trauma.

A fool's mouth is a self-made trap, their words a tight slap.

Gossip tastes like gourmet bites, sinking deep, out of sight.

Slacking in your work? You're wrecking it,
brother, not far from a wrecker.

The name of the Lord is a solid hideout, the
righteous run into and shout out.

Wealth feels like a fortress for the rich,
their high wall, in their pitch.

Pride comes before the fall, humility's the prelude to standing tall.

Jumping in before hearing out? That's folly, wrapped in doubt.

A strong spirit can carry you through, but
who can lift a spirit that's blue?

A smart heart hunts knowledge, wise ears
head towards wisdom's edge.

Your gift can open doors wide, leading you into the VIP side.

You might think you've got it right, until
another comes and sets it tight.

Disputes get chilled by casting lots, settling
beefs in even the hottest spots.

A wounded brother is a fortress untaken,
disputes are barriers unshaken.

You are what you eat, or so they say, words
can feed or lead you astray.

Life and death hang on the tongue's sway, you'll
reap the rewards of what you say.

Finding a partner is hitting the jackpot,
earning favor from the top spot.

The poor plead with tears in their eyes, the
rich respond with cold goodbyes.

Counting on friends might let you down, sometimes
a friend sticks closer than a sibling found.

CHAPTER XIX. VIBES OF WISDOM VS. FOOL'S FOLLY

Living honest on a budget beats lying through your teeth.

Rushing with no sense, you're bound to
trip, slow your roll, don't leap.

Messing up and blaming life? Nah, that's
on you, don't blame the skies.

Wealth makes you a magnet for friends,
poverty, even your shadow flies.

A liar's fate is sealed, no escape when truth is revealed.

Everyone's buddy when you're on top, gifts open doors non-stop.

Poor folks get the cold shoulder, even from
their own, no love, just colder.

Loving wisdom is self-love, keep it close, treasure trove.

Lies lead to a dead end, truth's the only trend.

Luxury ain't for fools, nor ruling for those who drool.

Cool heads prevail, forgiving wins without fail.

King's wrath roars like a lion, his favor, refreshing, no denying.

A foolish son is a father's despair, a nagging
spouse, a leaky nightmare.

Inheritance might give you a start, but a wise

partner comes from the heart.

Laziness invites deep sleep, hunger strikes when you don't leap.

Obeying rules is life's guard, ignore them, and life hits hard.

Helping the needy, you lend to the divine,
blessings come back, time after time.

Discipline your kid while there's hope, don't
set them on a slippery slope.

A hot head pays the price, try to chill, that's my advice.

Listen up, take the lesson, wisdom's path is a future blessing.

Man plans, but the Lord's will stands, it's His call across all lands.

Trustworthiness over wealth, honesty's the real stealth.

Fear the Lord, live full days, chasing sleep, life decays.

Too lazy to feed yourself? That's a path to nowhere, stealth.

Mock the mocker, wisdom's seen, teach the
wise, their minds are keen.

Disrespecting parents is a shame, a disgraceful claim to fame.

If you ignore all advice, you'll wander off, paying the price.

Lies and deceit, the wicked feast, but justice
finds them, to say the least.

Scorners and fools, they've got their match, a
good whipping, lesson attached.

CHAPTER XX. CHILL VIBES VS. BAD VIBES

Chilling with wine or beer leads to trouble, it's like playing with fire, you're bound to stumble.

Pissing off the king is a no-go, it's like facing a lion, a dangerous show.

Stepping away from drama is the real win, diving into fights is a foolish sin.

Being lazy when it counts just sets you up for falls, when harvest time comes, you'll have nothing in your halls.

Deep plans in a person's heart are like the ocean's mystery, but a smart soul dives deep, making history.

Lots talk a big game of loyalty and trust, but finding someone who's real? That's a must.

A righteous life blesses your kids with more than gold, doing right sets a legacy untold.

A king with justice clears all the evil under the sky, with just one look, wickedness says goodbye.

Claiming "I'm pure" is self-deception at its best, it's a question that puts your integrity to the test.

Even kids show their true face, whether their actions will be their grace or disgrace.

The Lord gives us ears to hear and eyes to see, catching

all of life's wonders, setting our spirits free.

Loving sleep a bit too much will leave you with nada,
open your eyes wide to enjoy your piñata.

"Bad deal," says the buyer, then brags when he's gone,
it's a game people play from dusk till dawn.

Real treasures aren't in gold or a heap of pearls,
but in wise words that unfurl.

Backing a stranger is like skating on thin ice,
securing your promise keeps things nice.

The bread of deceit might taste oh so sweet, but
later it turns to gravel, a deceitful treat.

Success comes when you plan with a crew, facing
battles alone? Nah, that won't do.

Spreading secrets is a gossip's favorite dish, keep
away if you wish to avoid this fish.

Cursing your parents brings darkness your way,
like walking blindfolded, every single day.

Quick gains at first might seem alright, but in
the end, they vanish from sight.

Thinking of revenge? Better to hold your peace,
trust in the Lord, and let the anger cease.

God hates cheating scales, it's just not right,
fairness in all things is His delight.

The Lord guides our steps, so why fret about your path?
Understanding life's plan is like doing complex math.

Making promises without thinking can trap you fast,
consider your vows, if you want them to last.

A wise king scatters the wicked with just one sweep,

like cleaning house, it's a promise he'll keep.

The human spirit is God's lamp, searching our
inner depths, it's like setting up camp.

Kindness and truth are the king's strong guard, on
these foundations, his reign is never hard.

Youth's pride is their strength, bold and bright, but
the elderly's silver hair is a beautiful sight.

Corrections might hurt, but they teach us what's right,
like cleansing wounds, bringing wisdom to light.

CHAPTER XXI. KING'S HEART AND GOD'S ART

A king's heart is like a stream in God's palm, He
guides it wherever, with a spiritual calm.

To each their path seems right, legit, but God's
the judge, on hearts He'll sit.

Fair play and truth over sacrifice, to God,
that's the ultimate life advice.

High and mighty, full of sin, their flashy light, it's wearing thin.

Hard work pays, haste makes waste, rushing
blindly, you'll miss the taste.

Lies for treasure, a fruitless chase, like
catching wind, a deadly race.

Violence takes the violent away, refusing
righteousness, they can't stay.

The wicked twist and turn, no straight line, but
the pure in heart, in truth they shine.

A quiet corner beats shared space, when
drama's served in endless grace.

Evil desires in a sinner's soul, blind to kindness, a heart not whole.

Correct a mocker, wisdom spreads, enlighten
one, knowledge treads.

The Righteous One watches the wicked's house,
turning it over, quiet as a mouse.

Ignore the poor, you'll cry alone, your calls
unanswered, like a stone.

A secret gift, anger's cure, a hidden hand, intentions pure.

Justice delights the good at heart, but to the evil, it's a dart.

Stray from sense, with shadows blend, a
path to darkness, a bitter end.

Party hard, wealth slips through, wine and oil, no riches due.

The wicked fall, the just stand tall, a traitor's end, justice for all.

Deserts better than a house of strife, with a
quarrelsome partner, draining life.

Wisdom's house is rich and grand, but fools
spend fast, can't understand.

Seeking goodness brings life and grace, with
honor and respect, you'll win the race.

Wisdom storms the mighty's gate, their
false security, a twisted fate.

Guard your words, keep peace in sight,
avoid the trouble, bask in light.

Boastful talk, a mocker's fame, ego unchecked, a dangerous game.

Laziness leads to a deep despair, but giving freely shows you care.

A bribe in secret turns the tide, but wicked
gifts, in shame they hide.

Liars fall, the wise will stand, speaking truth, a strong command.

The shameless show their face outright,

but the just will walk in light.

No wisdom or advice can sway, God's plan, on the final day.

Prepare for battle, do your part, but victory
comes from God's own heart.

CHAPTER XXII. RESPECT OVER RICHES

Respect trumps wealth, acceptance over gold and silver vibes.

The rich and poor meet, same Creator, no lies.

The wise see trouble and bounce, the clueless
crash and burn, no surprise.

Humility and fear of God, that's the wealth, respect, and life prize.

Thorns and traps on the wicked's path, stay
clear to keep your life on the rise.

Train up a kid right, and they won't stray,
even when they're old and wise.

The rich rule over the poor, borrowers
serve the lenders, no disguise.

Sow evil, reap trouble, the anger stick disappears before your eyes.

Blessed are those who are kind, sharing
bread with the poor is wise.

Kick out the mocker, peace comes in, where argument dies.

Lovers of purity of heart, their lips speak
persuasively, they win the king's ties.

God's eyes keep knowledge in check, but the liar's words He defies.

The lazy say, "There's a lion outside!" Excuses
for not trying, no surprise.

Deep pits, the adulteress's lips, God's wrath
makes them the unwise.

Folly is bound up in a child's heart, discipline
drives it away, no more lies.

Oppressing the poor to enrich oneself, giving
to the rich, leads to their demise.

WORDS OF THE WISE

Listen up, tune into wisdom, let it be known
on your lips, inside it flies.

To place your trust in the Lord, I'm pointing
you right, no disguise.

Didn't I pen you a triple treat of advice and
insight, for your life's ties?

To teach you truth and right, so you can
stand tall, in the sender's eyes.

Don't rob the poor or crush the needy, for God defends their cries.

Avoid the hot-headed, don't get entangled,
lest their temper be your demise.

Don't be among those who guarantee debts,
or your bed might be the prize.

Don't move ancient landmarks set by your
ancestors, that's where wisdom lies.

See someone skilled in their work? They'll stand
before kings, not just regular guys.

CHAPTER XXIII. CHILL VIBES VS. WILD TIMES

Chill with the big shots, watch what's in front of you; if
you're about that hungry life, maybe think twice.

Craving those fancy dishes? Nah, it's all an illusion, skip the chase.

Riches vanish like a snap, turning wings, flying
high - out of sight, out of grace.

Don't dine with the stingy; their treats aren't sweet. "Eat,
drink!" they say, but their heart's not in it, just deceit.

You'll regret those bites, wasting your kind words, all in vain.

Ignore fools, they trash wisdom, your words down the drain.

Don't cross ancient lines, don't mess with the
orphans' field, it's a no-go zone,

Their defender's strong, got their back,
turning your plans to stone.

Tune into wisdom, keep smart chats close, that's the way.

Don't spare the rod, no harm done, it's for
their soul, you'll save the day.

When wisdom fills your heart, it's all joy and pride inside,

Speaking what's right, making hearts light, on truth we ride.

Don't envy sinners, stick to fearing God, that's the real quest,

For sure, there's a future, your hope's not a jest.

Listen, my son, walk straight, keep your heart in the game,

Not with those who love booze or meat to their shame.

For drunkards and gluttons wear rags, living in blame.

Honor your parents, the ones who gave you your name.

Buy truth, wisdom, discipline, don't sell,
they're your claim to fame.

A wise son brings joy, so make your folks glad,

Give them your heart, let your eyes follow my pad.

Beware the seductress, a deep pit, the foreigner's a narrow well,

Lurking like a thief, multiplying the unfaithful, casting a spell.

Who has woes? Who has sorrows? Who's
got strife, who's got complaints?

Those lingering over wine, always in the tavern, no saints.

Don't be lured by wine's sparkle, how smoothly it goes down,

In the end, it bites like a snake, spreading poison around.

You'll see bizarre things, speak nonsense, feeling upside down,

Like sleeping in the sea or on a mast's top, bound to drown.

"They hit me, I felt nothing, when will I wake to go round again?"

Chasing that drink, never learning, stuck in the same refrain.

CHAPTER XXIV. REAL TALK FOR THE REAL WORLD

Don't envy the bad guys or crave their company because they're all about plotting trouble and talking trash.

Building a life? Wisdom's your architect, and smarts make it sturdy; knowledge fills the rooms with all things precious and sweet.

Brains over brawn any day. A clever strategist wins wars with wise counsel, not muscle.

Wisdom's too high for fools; they can't even open their mouths at the city gates where the real talk happens.

Plotting evil earns you the name 'troublemaker.'

If you're weak during tough times, then you're really weak.

Saving those being dragged to death? If you pretend you don't see, the One who guards souls notices and pays back accordingly.

Honey's sweet, so is wisdom for your life—it promises you a future, so your hope won't be cut off.

Don't wait outside the good guy's house, wrecking their place; because even if the righteous fall, they get up, but trouble is the end for the wicked.

Enjoying someone's downfall? Not cool. God might see and disapprove, turning His wrath away from them.

Don't stress over evildoers or be jealous; they don't

have a future, their light's going out.

Fear God and the king, my child, and steer clear
of rebels, for disaster strikes them fast.

Being fair in court is a must. Saying a criminal is innocent?
Expect the people's curse and nations' scorn.

But those who correct the wrongdoer will
be blessed with good things.

A straight answer feels like a kiss on the lips.

Finish your outdoor work and get your fields
ready; after that, build your house.

Don't accuse someone for no reason—would
you use your words to deceive?

No "they hurt me, so I'll hurt them back."
God will take care of the revenge.

I walked by a lazy person's farm and a fool's vineyard; thorns and
weeds everywhere, and the stone wall was broken down. I took
one look and got the message: Just a little sleep, a little slumber,
a little folding of the hands to rest—and poverty will jump on
you like a bandit; scarcity will attack you like an armed robber.

CHAPTER XXV. DON'T TRY TO BE A BIG SHOT

These are more proverbs from Solomon, copied by King Hezekiah's crew.

It's divine to keep secrets, but kings get glory for uncovering them. Like the sky's height or the ocean's depth, you can't figure out what kings are thinking.

Separate the bad vibes from the good, and you'll shine. Kick the troublemakers out, and the kingdom stands strong on justice.

Don't try to flex at the high table. Better to be invited up than sent packing in front of the big shots.

If you've seen something, don't rush to court. What's your move when your opponent makes you look foolish?

Sort out your beef without airing dirty laundry. Nobody wants their secrets blasted because then you're the one who ends up looking bad.

Right words at the right time? Pure gold. A wise correction to someone listening? Priceless.

A reliable messenger is as refreshing as snow in harvest time, cheering up their boss. But all talk and no action? That's just hot air.

Patience can break through to the top dog, and a gentle word can crush the toughest opposition.

Found honey? Eat just enough. Overdo it, and you'll regret it.

Don't wear out your welcome at your buddy's house.
Too much, and they'll start dreading your visits.

Lying about your neighbor? You might as well be attacking them.

Relying on someone unreliable in tough times? Like
walking on a broken foot or chewing with a bad tooth.

Singing happy songs to a heavy heart? That's as
welcome as stealing someone's coat in winter.

Feed your hungry enemy, and you'll heap coals on
their head. Yeah, you'll be the better person, and
who knows? Maybe you'll even get a reward.

Gossip spreads trouble like wildfire. Better to live alone in
a tiny attic than share a mansion with a drama queen.

Good news from afar? It's like that first sip
of water when you're parched.

Standing down in front of the wicked? It's like
a muddied spring or a ruined well.

Too much of a good thing, like honey, isn't great.
And remember, humility over pride, always.

A person without self-control? Like a city
broken into, defenseless.

CHAPTER XXVI. DON'T PLAY THE FOOL

Giving props to fools? That's like snow in summer, rain during harvest - totally out of place.

Words can't touch you without cause, like birds dodging and weaving, totally unfazed.

Some need a whip, others a bridle, but fools? They just need a good reality check.

Don't stoop to their level, play it cool, or you might just end up looking like a wreck.

But sometimes, you gotta show them their folly, so they don't get too cocky thinking they're wise.

Sending a message through a fool? That's like cutting off your feet, expect no prize.

Proverbs in the mouth of a fool? That's as shaky as a lame man's legs, makes no sense.

Honoring a fool? Might as well tie a rock to a slingshot - it's just dense.

A proverb in a fool's mouth? It stings like a thorn - totally misplaced, brings no light.

Hiring a fool or some drunk? You're asking for trouble, like an archer not aiming right.

Fools repeating their folly? It's like a dog returning

to its vomit, a sickening sight.

Think you're the smartest? More hope for a fool
than for you, that's the real insight.

"The lion's out there!" cries the lazy, finding
excuses not to move, stuck in their fear.

Just like doors swing on their hinges, the lazy
turn in their beds, never getting near.

Too lazy to feed themselves? It's like a journey too
far, just to bring the hand to the mouth.

Thinks he's wiser than seven wise advisors?
That's a lazy fool talking, no doubt.

Messing in others' drama? That's like grabbing a
stray dog by the ears - expect to get bit.

Joking about hurting others? It's no game. "Just
kidding!" doesn't cut it, not one bit.

Without gossip, conflicts die down, like a fire
without wood, it simply fades away.

Troublemakers kindle strife, but without
them, peace can finally sway.

Gossip's sweet but it sinks deep, causing harm
where it lands, spreading wide.

Flattering lips with a wicked heart? Like cheap
makeup on a clay pot, it can't hide.

A hater disguising with his lips, while plotting
in the heart, brings only pain.

Though malice hides, its wickedness will out,
in the crowd, it can't contain.

Dig a pit, you'll fall in it; roll a stone, it rolls

back. It's the karma train.

A lying tongue hates its victims, and smooth
talk leads only to ruin, leaving a stain.

CHAPTER XXVII. CHILL VIBES AND WISE VIBES

Don't flex about tomorrow, 'cause you don't
know what it's gonna show.

Let others hype you up, keep your own lips low.

Rocks are heavy, sand's a drag, but a fool's
anger? That's the heaviest bag.

Anger's fierce, jealousy's a flood, who can
stand when it's in the blood?

Open rebuke is way better than hidden love that's not shown.

Friend's wounds come from care, enemy's kisses are just for show.

Full stomach tramples honey, but to the
hungry, even bitterness is money.

Like a bird wandering from its nest, is a person
straying from their home, feeling unrest.

Fragrance and advice cheer the heart, just like
kind words that never depart.

Don't ditch your buddy or your dad's friend; in tough
times, on yourself, you can't just depend.

Get wise, kid, make my heart glad, so I can clap
back at those who make me mad.

See trouble coming? Better hide away. Fools keep going and pay.

No shirt? That's what you get for backing a stranger, and doing it again just puts you in danger.

Bless your neighbor loudly in the morning, might as well be calling them out, consider this a warning.

A nagging spouse on a rainy day, like trying to catch oil, they just won't stay away.

Iron sharpens iron, friends shape each other, it's all about giving, not what you smother.

Tend to your fig tree, enjoy its snack, look out for your boss, and they'll have your back.

We reflect others just like water face to face, in our hearts, it's our friends we can trace.

Death and destruction are never full, just like our eyes, always on the pull.

Gold and silver are tested by fire, but it's praise that reveals our true desire.

Even if you grind a fool in with grain, their foolishness will surely remain.

Look after your livestock, they're your true wealth, with them in good shape, you're assured of your health.

Wealth isn't forever, nor is a crown that passes through the town.

When the grass pops up and the herbs are seen, it's time to feed the animals green.

Sheep for your clothes, goats to buy land, plenty of goat's milk, for your household to stand.

CHAPTER XVIII. REAL TALK FOR THE BOLD HEART

Wicked run when no one's chasing, but the righteous stand bold as lions, embracing.

In sin's chaos, leaders are many, but wisdom and insight can bring peace aplenty.

Oppressors make rain that no bread provides, a storm leaving hunger that deeply divides.

Dis the Law, you cheer for the sinner; uphold it, you're the real winner.

Evil folks don't get what's just, but those seeking the Lord truly must.

A poor man walking the straight line beats a rich man's crooked design.

Law followers are wise sons indeed, while those who party bring their dads to plead.

Growing wealth through interest and gain, it's saved for those who the poor sustain.

Turn a deaf ear to the law's call, even prayers become an abhorrent downfall.

Lead the righteous astray, and you'll fall into the pit; for the pure, goodness is what they'll inherit.

Rich thinks he's smart, all on his own, but the

poor with insight really have grown.

When the righteous triumph, there's joy and cheer;
when the wicked rise, everyone hides in fear.

Hide your sins, you won't prosper, my friend; confess
and leave them, find mercy in the end.

Blessed is he who always fears the Lord, but the
hard-hearted will surely be floored.

A tyrant ruling the poor is a roaring lion or a hungry
bear, a ruler without compassion, a nightmare.

A prince lacking judgment is a high price to pay, but
those who hate dishonest gain will see a longer day.

A man guilty of another's blood will run till he
falls; let no one help him, as justice calls.

Walk the straight path and find your protection; stray
into wickedness, and you'll face correction.

Work the land, you'll have plenty to eat; chase
fantasies, and you'll find defeat.

A faithful man will abound with blessings, but
rush to riches, and you'll face distressings.

It's wrong to show favoritism, indeed; a man
would sin for a piece of bread in greed.

A greedy man hurries for wealth, not seeing
that poverty will come by stealth.

Correcting others will later be praised, more
than a flatterer who's always phased.

Robbing parents and claiming it's right is
partnering with thieves, out of sight.

A greedy heart stirs conflict, it's clear, but trusting

the Lord means you've nothing to fear.

Trusting in oneself is foolishness's sign;
wisdom's path leads to the divine.

Helping the poor means you won't lack, but
ignore them, and curses will stack.

When the wicked rise, people hide away, but
when they fall, the righteous will sway.

CHAPTER XXIX. LIFE'S TWISTS AND TRUTHS

A stubborn dude, despite the warnings, will crash
and burn, no chance of reforming.

When the righteous lead, the people cheer, but
when the wicked rule, everyone's in fear.

Loving wisdom makes your dad proud, hanging
with trouble, you'll lose your shroud.

A king with justice strengthens the nation, but
one who loves bribes brings devastation.

Flattery sets traps where you step, but honesty
builds bridges that are prepped.

The sin of the wicked is a deadly snare, but the
righteous sing and dance without a care.

The just know the needs of the poor, the
wicked's ignorance shows their core.

The town's in turmoil when the wicked lead, but the
righteous calm the storm with their deed.

Argue with a fool, and there's noise and sneers,
with no resolution in sight, just jeers.

Bloodthirsty hate the upright man, but the
righteous care for their lifespan.

A fool vents all his anger in a flash, but the

wise hold back, avoiding the clash.

When liars rule, the court's a mess, truth
brings order and success.

The poor meet the oppressor; God lights both
their ways, showing that justice plays.

A king who's fair will have a throne that lasts,
showing that virtue outcasts.

Discipline gives wisdom, don't let it slide; it
saves your kid from a shameful tide.

Increase in the wicked, increase in sin, but the
righteous will see their downfall and win.

Don't spoil your servant; they'll end up a foe,
correct them early so respect they'll show.

Anger causes fights; a hot temper's a curse, but
patience soothes, turning things inverse.

A king judges the land with truth in hand, ensuring
his kingdom will grandly stand.

Spare the rod, spoil the child, discipline saves them from the wild.

Without a vision, the people perish, but happy
is he who the law does cherish.

Words won't train up; actions are required,
otherwise, rebellion is acquired.

Talk too much? More likely to err, silence
is golden, as wise men prefer.

A quick-tempered man stirs up strife, but
trusting in God brings a peaceful life.

Many seek the ruler's favor; it's clear, but
justice for all is God's premier.

The wicked and the righteous, two opposite poles,
each detested by the other's souls.

CHAPTER XXX. AGUR'S LIFE HACKS

Yo! Agur here, just a regular dude talking to Itiel and the crew, spilling the tea on life, wisdom, and the universe.

So, I'm not exactly the brainiest in the group. Wisdom and divine knowledge? Yeah, not my forte. But here's what I've been pondering:

Who's got the whole world in their hands? Who's zipping up to heaven and back like it's NBD? Who's got the wind on speed dial, or wrapping up the oceans like it's a to-go order? And who set the world's edges like it's a giant game of Minecraft? Got a name for this dude? How 'bout his kid's name? Anyone? Bueller?

God's words are pure gold, a bulletproof vest for the soul. Mess with them, and you're asking for a world of hurt. Here's what I'm begging for before I peace out of this life: Keep me from lying and fake news. Don't let me get too rich or hit rock bottom. Just give me enough grub to keep me going. Too much cash might make me forget who's boss, and too little might push me into doing something stupid, throwing shade on God's name.

Don't be throwing your squad under the bus in front of their boss. That's just asking for a curse to come your way.

There's a crowd out there cursing their dads and dissing their moms. Clean on the outside but filthy inside. Walking around like they own the place, but they're just looking to tear down the needy.

Bloodsuckers got two daughters, always screaming, "Gimme! Gimme!" Just like death, the barren womb, parched earth, and fire —never saying, "Enough."

Those who diss their folks, expect the ravens to come calling or eagles to drop by for a snack.

Here are some head-scratchers for you: How does an eagle glide through the sky, a snake slither on a rock, a ship navigate the ocean, or how dudes vibe with their crushes? And then there's the chick who eats, wipes her mouth, and is like, "What? I didn't do anything wrong."

Some things just shake up the earth and can't handle the heat: A nobody turning into a somebody overnight, a fool stuffed with food, a hated woman finally getting her ring, and a maid taking over her mistress's spot.

And now, for the tiny but mighty crew of the animal kingdom: Ants—no muscle but all hustle in the summer; rock badgers— weak but home is where the heart (and safety) is; locusts—no king but moving in sync; and lizards—catching those palace vibes without a care.

Some walk with swagger: lions, roosters, goats, and a king with his people. Got too big for your britches? Better to cover that mouth before you eat those words. Stirring up trouble? Expect trouble to stir you up right back.

And that's the word according to Agur—slices of wisdom pie served with a side of humility and a reality check. Keep it real, fam. Peace!

CHAPTER XXXI. LEMUEL'S LIFE HACKS

Words from Lemuel, a king raised by a queen with wisdom. She's like, "What's up, my son? What's up, my promise to the world?"

MOTHER'S TEACHINGS

"Don't waste your strength chasing those who might ruin kings. It's not all about that life."

"Yo, Lemuel, kings shouldn't be drowning in wine or craving that strong drink. That's how you forget what's right and twist the rules for those who can't stand up for themselves."

"Give strong drink to those who are lost, and wine to those with heavy hearts. Let them drink to forget their poverty and remember their misery no more."

"Be the voice for the voiceless, the defender of the downtrodden. Stand for justice and speak for the rights of the needy and poor."

AN ODE TO THE VIRTUOUS WOMAN

Finding a virtuous woman? Priceless. Her partner trusts her completely, never needing to chase wealth.

She brings the good, not harm, all the days of her life. Grinding from day to night, she's the early bird getting that bread, serving up food and directions like a boss.

She considers investments wisely, planting vineyards with her own hands, showcasing her strength and determination.

She sees the value in her work; her light shines bright 24/7. Skilled in crafts, generous at heart, always ready for the worst weather, looking fly in fine linen and purple.

Her partner's respected, known in the community. She makes and sells linen garments, bringing her own flavor to the marketplace.

Strength and dignity are her vibe, laughing without fear of the future, dropping wisdom, and kindness every time she speaks.

Watching over her household, she's not about that lazy life. Her kids and partner give her props, saying she's the real MVP.

While some excel in one way, she surpasses them all. Beauty fades, but a woman who respects the Lord deserves praise.

Give her credit for her hard work, let her achievements be her shoutout.

LEMUEL'S MOM DROPS THE MIC

"Don't chase after the wrong things or let the good times distract you from what really matters. Stand up for those who can't and live with integrity. Remember, a woman who fears the Lord is to be praised."

63503103R10046